Lisa Nieschlag Lars Wentrup

TASTE THE WILD

RECIPES AND STORIES FROM CANADA

Food photography
Lisa Nieschlag

Photography Canada
Sascha Talke

Recipe development
Verena Poppen

murdoch books
Sydney | London

IN SEARCH OF SPACE
A new day dawns

LIMITLESS FREEDOM
An adventure begins

Contents

20   French toast with lemon sugar

23   Breakfast wraps with scrambled eggs

24   Pumpkin spice muffins

27   Grilled avocado with tomato chutney

30   Peanut butter and chocolate granola

33   Almond porridge with cranberry sauce

38   Waffles with salted butterscotch sauce

41   Blueberry pancakes with maple syrup

42   Wild rice frittata with mushrooms and bacon

45   White hot chocolate

52   Berry latte

59   Pan-baked Bannock pizza

60   Springtime potato salad

63   No-knead bread

64   Grilled cheese sandwich

71   Prawn skewers with sriracha dip

72   One-pot mac & cheese

75   Tourtière

80   Beaver bites

83   Butter tarts

88   Nanaimo bars

STORIES

Anne Michaels **Fugitive pieces**   12

Margaret Atwood **Uncles**   49

Charles Dickens **In Canada**   84

Chris Czajkowski **Cabin at Singing River**   167

GO YOUR OWN WAY
Live the moment

BLISSFUL SOLITUDE
Campfires under the stars

97 Lobster roll

98 Poutine

101 Ink-black halibut burgers

102 Clam chowder

105 Seafood risotto

110 Chicken and mushroom pot pie

113 Pear salad with grilled scallops

114 Mayonnaise

115 Barbecue sauce

119 Smoked trout

120 Chocolate pudding cake

123 Cinnamon scrolls with bacon

124 Home-made iced tea with cranberries

127 Toasted crostini with blueberries

134 Cauldron goulash with pale ale

137 Onion campfire bread with Cajun spice butter

138 Baked potatoes with herbed sour cream and salmon

141 Pulled pork burgers

146 Grilled corn with chipotle mayonnaise

149 Warm grilled vegetable salad

152 Maple-glazed spare ribs

155 Whisky roast chicken

158 Cedar plank salmon fillet

161 Roast beef with smashed potatoes

163 S'mores

173 Marinated bananas with hazelnuts and meringue

174 Maple cheesecake with strawberries

177 Grilled lemonade/Caesar

Wanderlust

Sascha Talke
Photography Canada

Ninja Talke

**Teamwork makes
the dream work.**

Lisa Nieschlag
Food photography

Lars Wentrup
Design

Canada has always been shaped by its unique nature. This is where one of the world's first national parks was created, and the country's seemingly limitless expanses of untouched wilderness still allow visitors to experience nature at its most pristine. In Canada, the snow seems whiter, the water clearer and the animals less disturbed than anywhere else in the world. It is the ultimate dream destination!

Who wouldn't want to set out into new, vast spaces, explore a wide and wild country, leave everyday life behind, venture into the unknown carrying nothing but a backpack, experience nature up close and immerse oneself in a wilderness adventure...

Whenever we talk and dream about nature-based travel, Canada is usually right at the top of people's lists, because it's the perfect place for treating yourself to a true sense of freedom. But why limit yourself to words and dreams, why not actually do it? Canada means meandering through vast forests in a campervan, going bear-watching, sitting next to a campfire and savouring every minute of every day. It's putting on a lumberjack shirt, tying up one's hiking boots, packing a bag of camping gear and heading off.

Venturing into Canada's wilderness on a big road trip is precisely what Sascha and his wife Ninja did. They travelled across this huge country and brought back a host of amazing memories and plenty of fantastic photos of awe-inspiring scenery. Their pictures set the scene for recipes inspired by the rich diversity of Canada's nature and people, who have migrated to this promised land from all over the world for centuries, shaping it in many different ways, but never quite taming it. The ingredients and flavours are drawn from a well of simplicity and ingenuity, abundance and restraint, and they tell stories of forests, rivers and lakes.

We have put together the recipes and photos in a cookbook that reflects Canada's heart and soul, expresses its expansive nature and brings its sense of adventure into our kitchens. This book leaves space for dreams. It celebrates simple pleasures and is inspired by a yearning for freedom and space. We hope that its recipes will flavour your home with a taste of wilderness.

Go your own way. Feel free, even if you don't have the time to travel – have this book deliver the essence of Canada to you.

Have fun exploring!

Lisa and Lars

ADVENTURES
START
WHERE PLANS
END.

FUGITIVE PIECES

Anne Michaels

When my parents came to Toronto, they saw that most of their fellow immigrants settled in the same downtown district: a rough square of streets from Spadina to Bathurst, Dundas to College, with waves of the more established rippling northward towards Bloor Street. My father would not make the same mistake. "They wouldn't even have the trouble of rounding us up."

Instead, my parents moved to Weston, a borough that was quite rural and separate from downtown. They took out a large mortgage on a small house by the Humber River.

Our neighbours soon understood my parents wanted privacy. My mother nodded a hello as she scurried in and out. My father parked as near as he could to the back door, which faced out onto the river, so he could avoid the neighbour's dog. Our major possessions were the piano and a car in decline. My mother's pride was her garden, which she arranged so the roses could climb the back wall of the house.

I loved the river, though my five-year-old explorations were held in close check by my mother; a barrage of clucks from the kitchen window if I even started to take off my shoes. Except for spring, the Humber was lazy, willows trailed the current. On summer nights, the bank became one long living room.

The water was speckled with porch lights. People wandered along it after dinner, children lay on their lawns listening to the water and waiting for the Big Dipper to appear. I watched from my bedroom window, too young to stay out. The night river was the colour of a magnet. I heard the muffled thump of a tennis ball in an old stocking against a wall and the faint chant of the girl next door: "A sailor went to sea sea sea, to see what he could see see see…" Except for the occasional slapping of a mosquito, the occasional shout of a child in a game that always seemed dusky far, the summer river was a muted string. It emanated twilight; everyone grew quiet around it.

My parents hoped that, in Weston, God might overlook them. 🍁

In search of space

Finding peace, expanding your horizon, making new discoveries and finding yourself all the while – this is what Canada allows you to do. Far away from digital media and everyday life. After all, the best stories are experienced offline.

Say yes to new adventures.

French toast – what better to make with not-so-fresh bread? In this Canadian-inspired version, lemon sugar replaces the usual cinnamon for an entirely new taste experience. By the way, the lemon sugar tastes amazing in tea, so don't hesitate to make a bigger batch!

French toast with lemon sugar

Makes 8 slices

400 ml (14 fl oz) milk
3 tbsp vanilla sugar
Grated zest of ½ lemon
2 large eggs
2 tbsp butter
8 slices day-old brioche

For the lemon sugar:
Grated zest of 1 lemon
½ cup (110 g) sugar

Also:
Icing (confectioners') sugar,
  for sprinkling
Grated zest of 1 lemon,
  for garnish

For the lemon sugar, stir the grated lemon zest and sugar together in a small bowl until well combined. This is best done a few days in advance to allow the full lemon flavour to develop. Store in an airtight container.

Whisk the milk with the vanilla sugar, grated lemon zest and eggs in a large, shallow bowl. Set aside.

Melt the butter in a frying pan over medium heat. Meanwhile, dip the brioche slices into the egg mixture for 15 seconds on each side. Transfer to the hot pan and fry until golden brown on each side. Be careful when flipping the toasts over, as they can fall apart easily. Add a little more butter to the pan as necessary.

Divide the toasts among plates in stacks to match your appetite and sprinkle generously with the lemon sugar. Dust with icing sugar and serve warm, garnished with grated lemon zest.

Canada's diversity also makes for a wonderfully varied breakfast culture. You'll find sweet dishes such as French toast, breakfast muffins and pancakes as well as savoury ones such as these wraps, which are quick and easy to prepare and provide plenty of energy for the day's adventures.

Breakfast wraps with scrambled eggs

Whisk the eggs, salt, pepper and paprika together in a mixing bowl. Rinse the chives, shake off excess water and slice finely. Set aside a little for garnish and stir the rest into the egg mixture. Transfer the mixture to a cold non-stick frying pan. Place the pan over medium heat and cook the eggs gently until set, using a spatula to push the mixture together in the middle of the pan for an even texture.

Briefly toast the tortillas on both sides in a chargrill pan. Remove from the pan, spread with the sour cream and top with the thinly sliced ham.

Divide the scrambled eggs among the tortillas and fold the tortillas in half. Garnish with chopped chives to taste and serve warm with cherry tomatoes.

Makes 4

12 eggs
Salt
Freshly ground black pepper
1 tsp sweet paprika
1 bunch chives
4 tortillas
⅔ cup (150 g) thick
    sour cream
200 g (7 oz) very thinly
    sliced ham

Also:
Cherry tomatoes, for serving

This recipe has developed from the culinary exchange between Canada and its neighbour – both Canadians and Americans love sweetening foods with pumpkin. Puréed pumpkin keeps well in the refrigerator for several days; simply transfer any leftovers to a clean container and use to make a pumpkin pie, for example.

Pumpkin spice muffins

Makes 12

800 g (1 lb 12 oz) pumpkin
2 cups (300 g) plain flour
3 tsp baking powder
1 tsp ground cinnamon
1 tsp ground cloves
½ tsp freshly grated nutmeg
½ tsp ground ginger
½ tsp allspice
½ tsp bicarbonate of soda
   (baking soda)
½ tsp salt
4 tbsp butter, softened
230 g (8 oz) sugar
2 tbsp coconut sugar
2 eggs, at room temperature
240 ml (8 fl oz) buttermilk
4 tbsp mild-flavoured
   vegetable oil

For the frosting:
250 g (9 oz) cream cheese
4 tbsp butter, softened
2 cups (250 g) icing
   (confectioners') sugar
1 tsp ground cinnamon
1 tsp vanilla extract

Preheat the oven to 190°C (375°F). Line a 12-hole muffin tin with paper cases.

Wash, trim and quarter the pumpkin and scrape out the seeds. Cut the quarters into 1 cm (½ inch) slices. Transfer to a baking tray lined with baking paper and bake for about 25 minutes or until soft. Remove from the oven and purée the pumpkin. Set aside 220 g (7¾ oz) of the pumpkin purée. Refrigerate or freeze the remainder for another recipe.

Combine the flour, baking powder, spices, bicarbonate of soda and salt in a large mixing bowl. In a separate bowl, whisk the butter, sugar and coconut sugar until creamy with an electric mixer. Add the eggs, one at a time, and whisk to combine. Stir in the buttermilk, reserved pumpkin purée and vegetable oil. Quickly fold in the dry ingredients. Divide the batter among the muffin holes.

Bake the muffins for about 25 minutes. Remove and set aside to cool for 5 minutes. Transfer the muffins to a wire rack and leave to cool completely.

For the frosting, combine the cream cheese and butter in a bowl. Stir in the sifted icing sugar, along with the cinnamon and vanilla. Spread each muffin with a little frosting.

Creamy avocados have been a firm favourite for a long time. If you're a savoury breakfast person, you'll love these warm, grilled avocados topped with a sweet-and-sour tomato chutney.

Grilled avocado with tomato chutney

For the chutney, wash and halve the tomatoes. Remove the stem bases and finely dice the flesh. Peel and finely dice the onion. Peel the mango, remove the stone and cut into small dice. Transfer the tomatoes, onion and mango to a small saucepan and gently cook until heated through and thickened. Remove from the heat. Season with cider vinegar and salt.

Halve the avocados lengthwise and remove the stones. Brush the tops with olive oil and transfer the avocados to a chargrill pan or barbecue plate, cut side down. Remove once they have softened and browned a little on the surface. Flip over and fill the holes with the tomato chutney.

Rinse the parsley and shake off excess water. Pick off the leaves and use to garnish the avocados before serving.

Serves 4

4 avocados
1 tbsp olive oil

For the chutney:
2 cups (300 g) cherry
   tomatoes
1 red onion
150 g (5½ oz) mango
2 tbsp apple cider vinegar
Salt

Also:
2 sprigs flat-leaf parsley,
   for garnish

**GOING TO
THE WOODS
IS GOING
HOME**

Granola is great at any time of the day, whether as a delicious breakfast cereal or as a crunchy sprinkle on yoghurt or ice cream. In its basic form, it is simply baked oats sweetened with sugar or honey, but granola is open to many variations. This recipe has added peanut butter and chocolate. If you like, you can also add some chopped hazelnuts or peanuts.

Peanut butter and chocolate granola

Makes 1 large jar

150 g (5½ oz) crunchy
   peanut butter
½ cup (180 g) honey
2 pinches salt
6 cups (600 g) traditional
   rolled oats
150 g (5½ oz) dark chocolate
   (50–60% cocoa)
150 g (5½ oz) milk chocolate

Preheat the oven to 180°C (350°F). Line a large baking tray with baking paper.

Combine the peanut butter, honey and salt in a saucepan and heat, stirring constantly, until the mixture turns liquid. Stir in the oats. Remove from the heat and spread the mixture evenly over the baking tray. Bake for about 15 minutes, until the oats are golden brown.

Meanwhile, coarsely chop both types of chocolate.

Remove the granola from the oven and set aside to cool for 10 minutes. Toss the chocolate with the granola. Set aside to cool completely for at least 2 hours. Transfer to an airtight jar for storage.

There's gruel and there's its modern cousin, delectably updated porridge. Porridge is prepared a little differently from one country to the next and served either hot or cold. This sweet version with vanilla and cinnamon goes very well with cranberry sauce and fresh berries.

Almond porridge with cranberry sauce

For the cranberry sauce, heat the orange juice and sugar in a saucepan, stirring, until the sugar has dissolved. Add the cranberries and briefly bring to the boil. Add the raspberries and simmer the sauce for 10 minutes over low heat. Dissolve the cornflour in a little cold water, then whisk into the sauce. Remove from the heat and set aside to cool a little.

Split the vanilla bean lengthwise and scrape out the seeds. Heat the almond milk in a saucepan over low heat. Remove from the heat, add the vanilla seeds and set aside to infuse for 10 minutes. Stir in the oats and cinnamon. Simmer over low heat, stirring occasionally, for 5 minutes until the porridge is creamy.

Mix in the almond butter and maple syrup. Divide the porridge among four bowls and serve topped with the cranberry sauce and fresh berries.

Serves 4

1 vanilla bean
4 cups (1 litre) almond milk
2½ cups (250 g) traditional rolled oats
1 tsp ground cinnamon
1 tbsp almond butter
Maple syrup, to taste

For the cranberry sauce:
230 ml (7¾ fl oz) orange juice
200 g (7 oz) sugar
340 g (11¾ oz) fresh or frozen cranberries
2 cups (250 g) fresh or frozen raspberries
1 tsp cornflour

Also:
500 g (1 lb 2 oz) fresh berries (strawberries, blueberries, blackberries)

Travel is
the healthiest
addiction.

LET'S FIND SOME
BEAUTIFUL PLACE
TO GET LOST

Whether with afternoon tea or as an indulgently sweet breakfast, waffles make a delightful treat at any time of the day. This recipe makes particularly fluffy waffles, which are served drizzled with a home-made butterscotch sauce. Canadians love their butterscotch as much as Australians love their mango.

Waffles with salted butterscotch sauce

Serves 4

1 vanilla bean
450 ml (16 fl oz) milk
1 tbsp sugar
200 g (7 oz) butter, melted,
   plus extra for greasing
8 eggs, separated
1⅔ cups (250 g) plain flour
1 pinch salt

For the butterscotch sauce:
400 g (14 oz) brown sugar
1.2 litres (42 fl oz) single
   (pure) cream
1 tsp salt

Also:
Raspberries, for serving

For the butterscotch sauce, caramelise the brown sugar in a small saucepan over medium heat, without stirring. Deglaze with the cream (be careful, the caramel will be very hot!) and simmer for about 5 minutes until you have a creamy caramel sauce (it will thicken further as it cools). Stir in the salt.

Preheat the waffle iron for the waffles. Split the vanilla bean lengthwise and scrape out the seeds. Combine the milk, sugar, vanilla seeds and melted butter. Whisk in the egg yolks. Sift the flour over the mixture and whisk until all lumps have dissolved. Beat the egg whites and salt in a large bowl until stiff. Gently fold into the batter.

Grease the waffle iron. Add one ladleful of batter at a time and cook the waffles until golden brown. Serve the waffles with the warm butterscotch sauce and fresh raspberries.

The ultimate breakfast across North America! Make these sweet breakfast pancakes on the thick and small side rather than thin and larger like crêpes. Canadian blueberries have a particularly intense flavour, especially those picked wild. The maple syrup drizzle on top is an absolute must!

Blueberry pancakes with maple syrup

Finely chop the white chocolate. Combine the flour with the baking powder, sugar, vanilla sugar and salt in a mixing bowl. Whisk the egg yolks with the milk and melted butter. Beat the egg whites until stiff. Add the egg mixture to the dry ingredients and stir to combine. Wash and pick through the blueberries and pat dry. Gently fold the chopped white chocolate and blueberries into the batter. Gently fold in the beaten egg whites. Set aside for 10 minutes until small bubbles start to form on the surface.

Heat a non-stick frying pan over medium heat and add a little butter. Ladle small portions of batter into the pan. Fry until the tops of the pancakes start to dry. Flip the pancakes over with a spatula and briefly brown on the second side.

Divide the pancakes among four plates and serve with a little butter, maple syrup and fresh blueberries.

Serves 4

200 g (7 oz) white chocolate
3¼ cups (480 g) plain flour
1 tbsp baking powder
150 g (5½ oz) sugar
1½ tbsp vanilla sugar
½ tsp salt
6 large eggs, separated
720 ml (24 fl oz) milk
170 g (5¾ oz) butter, melted, plus extra for greasing and for serving
1⅔ cups (250 g) fresh blueberries

Also:
Maple syrup, for serving
Blueberries, for serving

With its delicate long grains and a nutty taste, wild rice is very different from plain rice in both appearance and taste. This shouldn't come as a surprise, as wild rice is actually the seeds of a wild reed grass that is not related to rice at all. It imparts a wonderful flavour to this frittata and makes it a satisfying meal.

Wild rice frittata with mushrooms and bacon

Serves 2

⅔ cup (125 g) wild rice
1 tsp salt
5 eggs
2 egg whites
3 sprigs parsley
½ tsp salt
½ tsp freshly ground
   black pepper
¼ tsp freshly grated
   nutmeg
1 red onion
2 tsp olive oil
1 sprig rosemary
200 g (7 oz) mixed
   mushrooms (chanterelles,
   button mushrooms)
3 small slices bacon
½ cup (45 g) grated
   parmesan

Place the wild rice in a sieve and rinse thoroughly in cold water. Transfer the rice and salt to a saucepan together with 230 ml (7¾ fl oz) water. Bring to the boil. Cover with a lid and simmer the rice over low heat for 40–50 minutes. Drain and set aside.

Whisk the eggs and egg whites in a bowl. Rinse the parsley and shake off excess water. Pick off the leaves and chop finely. Stir the parsley, salt, pepper and nutmeg into the egg mixture. Peel and finely dice the onion. Heat the olive oil in an ovenproof frying pan. Add the onion and sweat until translucent. Rinse the rosemary and shake off excess water. Pick off the leaves and add to the onion. Wipe the mushrooms with a clean tea towel and halve. Transfer to the pan, increase the heat to high and sear. Reduce the heat and add the wild rice.

Preheat the oven using the grill function. Pour the egg mixture into the pan and allow to set over low heat. Top with the bacon and parmesan. Transfer the pan to the oven and bake the frittata under the grill for about 5 minutes.

There's nothing more comforting than snuggling under a cosy blanket on your sofa with a mug of hot chocolate – best, of course, with a view of Canada's wide-open spaces. If that's not an option, this hot white chocolate spiced with nutmeg, cinnamon and cardamom is also ideal for soothing any aching desires to travel.

White hot chocolate

Coarsely chop the white chocolate and set aside.

Heat the sugar in a saucepan until caramelised to a golden-brown colour. Do not stir. Add the milk and simmer until any lumps have dissolved. Remove the saucepan from the heat and stir in the white chocolate and spices. Stir briefly and divide among four mugs.

Serve topped with marshmallows.

Serves 4

200 g (7 oz) white chocolate
4 tbsp sugar
4 cups (1 litre) milk
1 tsp ground cinnamon
1 pinch ground cardamom
1 pinch freshly grated nutmeg

Also:
Marshmallows, for serving

**We have nothing
to lose and
a world to see.**

Margaret Atwood

It was the aunts who brought most of the food for the Sunday dinners. They would arrive with roasts, lemon meringue pies, cookies, jars of their own pickles. Her mother might cook some potatoes, or make a jellied salad. Not a great deal was expected of her, because she was a war widow; she was still getting over the loss, and she had a child to bring up single-handed. On the outside it didn't seem to bother her. She was cheerful and rounded, and slow-moving by nature. The uncles had clubbed together to buy her the house, because she was their little sister, they had all grown up on a farm together, they were close.

The aunts had a hard time forgiving this. It would come up at the dinner table, in oblique references to how you had to scrimp to meet two sets of mortgage repayments. The uncles would look at their wives with baffled reproach, and pass their plates down to Susanna's mother for another helping of mashed potatoes. You could not turn your own flesh and blood out on the streets to starve. Susanna knew this because she heard an uncle saying it as he lumbered down the front walk to his car.

"You didn't have to get such a big house," the aunt said. "It's almost as big as ours." Her high heels clipped on the cement as she hurried to keep up. All of the aunts were small, brisk women, with short legs.

Susanna was rocking in the giant wicker rocker on the porch. She stopped rocking and scrunched down so her head was out of sight, to listen in.

"Come on, Adele," said the uncle. "You wouldn't want them living in a hut."

"She could get a job." This was an insult and the aunt knew it. It would mean that the uncle could not provide.

"Who would look after Susanna?" said the uncle, coming to a stop while he hunted for his keys. "Not you, that's for sure."

There was a note of bitterness in the uncle's voice that was new to Susanna. She felt sorry for him. For the aunt she felt no pity. 🍁

This latte is supercharged with berries. If kept in a sterilised bottle or jar, the berry coulis will keep for several days in the refrigerator, so don't hesitate to make a larger quantity. Feel free to experiment with different ratios of almond and coconut milk until you find your favourite.

Berry latte

Serves 2

⅔ cup (100 g) frozen
  blueberries
1 cup (100 g) frozen
  cranberries
1 Rooibos tea bag
2 tbsp maple syrup
1 tsp ground ginger
1 tsp ground cardamom
2 tbsp vanilla sugar
150 ml (5 fl oz) almond milk
100 ml (3½ fl oz) coconut
  milk

Also:
Ground cinnamon,
  for dusting

Add the blueberries and cranberries to a saucepan with 115 ml (3¾ fl oz) water. Immerse the tea bag in the liquid, add the maple syrup, ginger, cardamom and vanilla sugar and bring to the boil. Reduce the heat and simmer for 5–10 minutes.

Remove the tea bag and squeeze out. Pass the berry mixture through a fine sieve and divide among two glasses.

Warm the almond and coconut milks and froth with a milk frother. Pour the milk over the berries and serve dusted with cinnamon.

Limitless freedom

The day has only started. You've chosen your route, and the adventure can begin. What will it bring? What experiences lie ahead of you in the wilderness? A feeling of tremendous freedom gradually mixes with curiosity about the unknown and respect for nature's unpredictability.

The best stories are
experienced offline.

Bannock flatbread is a true classic of outdoor cooking, which can be prepared just as easily over a campfire as over a gas cooker. In this recipe, it is used as the base for two delicious pan-baked takes on pizza.

Pan-baked Bannock pizza

For the tomato sauce, peel and finely mince the garlic. Heat the olive oil in a small saucepan and briefly fry the garlic. Add the passata and bring to the boil. Pick the thyme and rosemary leaves and chop finely. Add the herbs, sugar and salt to the sauce and simmer for 30 minutes over low heat.

Combine the ingredients for the pizza dough in a mixing bowl with 1 cup (250 ml) water until you have a pliable dough.

For version 1, rinse the basil and pat dry. For version 2, peel and quarter the pumpkin. Scrape out the seeds with a spoon. Use a vegetable peeler to thinly slice the pumpkin. Heat the olive oil in a frying pan. Add the sliced pumpkin and sweat over medium heat.

Remove the dough from the bowl and knead energetically on a lightly floured surface until it is pliable. Divide the pizza dough into 8 portions and roll out very thinly with a rolling pin.

Brush a non-stick frying pan with a little olive oil. Add the flatbreads, one at a time, cover and toast over medium heat. Flip over once the bottom starts to take on colour and turn off the heat. Spread the bread with some of the tomato sauce and your choice of topping. Wait until the second side has also browned, then remove from the pan. Repeat with the remaining flatbreads.

Makes 8

For the tomato sauce:
2 garlic cloves
2 tbsp olive oil
500 g (1 lb 2 oz) jar tomato
  passata (puréed tomatoes)
1 sprig thyme
1 sprig rosemary
1½ tsp sugar
Salt

For the pizza dough:
3 cups (450 g) plain flour,
  plus extra for dusting
4 tbsp olive oil, plus extra
  for greasing
Salt

Version 1:
1 bunch basil
250 g (9 oz) ricotta
200 g (7 oz) thinly sliced
  salami

Version 2:
200 g (7 oz) pumpkin
1 tbsp olive oil
250 g (9 oz) ricotta
2 cups (100 g) baby English
  spinach

What's so fabulous about potato salad is that it can make both a scrumptious side and a filling main. Potato salad tastes best with home-made mayonnaise. Feel free to vary the recipe, adding bacon, pickled cucumbers or asparagus depending on the season and your personal taste.

Springtime potato salad

Serves 4

1 kg (2 lb 4 oz) small new
  potatoes
Salt
1 bunch radishes with
  greens attached
1 bunch chives
300 g (10½ oz) asparagus
2 tbsp olive oil
Freshly ground black pepper
¾ cup (50 g) alfalfa sprouts

For the dressing:
150 g (5½ oz) mayonnaise
  (see p. 114)
100 g (3½ oz) Greek-style
  yoghurt

Thoroughly scrub the potatoes. Halve each, transfer to a large saucepan and boil in salted water until done, for about 35 minutes. Drain the potatoes and leave to cool completely.

For the dressing, whisk the mayonnaise and yoghurt together and set aside.

Rinse the radishes and chives and pat dry. Trim off the radish greens and root tips. Set aside the greens. Finely chop the chives and halve the radishes. Trim or peel any woody asparagus ends. Cut the asparagus into bite-sized pieces.

Heat some olive oil in a frying pan and briefly fry the radishes and asparagus. Gently toss the vegetables with the dressing, potatoes and chives. Season with salt and pepper and serve garnished with alfalfa sprouts and radish greens.

For a mere five minutes' work, this dough will reward you with a delicious, crusty loaf. The dough does not need any kneading – it is simply folded before baking.

No-knead bread

Combine the dry ingredients in a large mixing bowl. Add the water and knead until well combined. Cover with plastic wrap and set aside to rise for 24 hours.

Once the dough has proven, remove it from the bowl and pull it into a wide rectangle on a lightly floured surface. Fold it over three times from one of the narrow sides. Shape the folded dough into a ball and place it on your lightly floured work bench, seam side down. Dust with flour, cover with a clean tea towel and leave to rise for 2 hours.

Meanwhile, preheat the oven to 250°C (500°F). Place a cast-iron roasting dish and lid in the hot oven to heat for about 30 minutes. Transfer the dough to the dish, seam side up. Cover with the lid and place in the hot oven. After 30 minutes, take the bread out of the dish and place it straight on the oven rack. Reduce the heat to 230°C (450°F) and bake for another 15 minutes. Leave to cool before slicing.

Makes 1 loaf

3⅓ cups (500 g) strong
   bread flour, plus extra
   for dusting
2 tsp salt
¼ tsp dry yeast
350 ml (12 fl oz) lukewarm
   water

Cranberries are popular all over the world but are native to Canada and the United States, which are also the main exporters. Whether fresh, dried or frozen, cranberries are a great addition to both sweet and savoury dishes and impart a uniquely fruity, tangy flavour. Here they deliver a fresh take on a classic grilled cheese toastie.

Grilled cheese sandwich

Makes 4

8 thick slices of bread
150 g (5½ oz) cranberry jam
    (or loganberry jam)
150 g (5½ oz) sliced cheddar
    cheese
150 g (5½ oz) mild gorgonzola
    cheese
4 jalapeños
2 tbsp ghee

Spread 4 slices of the bread with cranberry jam and top with the cheddar and gorgonzola. Slice the jalapeños into rings and divide among the bread. Top with another slice of bread each.

Heat the ghee in a frying pan over medium heat. Fry the toasties until golden brown on one side. Cover with a lid while frying to ensure that the cheese melts nicely. Flip the sandwiches over and fry on the second side until golden brown. Cut the toasties into triangles and serve warm.

When I am in Canada, I feel this is what the world should be like.

Canada actually supplies most of the world's prawns. Prawns are very easy to prepare – simply add a little oil, salt and lemon juice to allow their own flavour to shine. They go incredibly well with this sriracha dip. These skewers are also excellent grilled.

Prawn skewers with sriracha dip

For the dip, wash, trim and finely dice the celery. Peel and coarsely dice the garlic. Sweat the celery and garlic in a small saucepan with the canola oil. Add the tomato passata and simmer for 15 minutes.

Purée the tomato mixture with a stick blender until smooth. Season with the sriracha sauce, honey, Worcestershire sauce, salt and pepper. Set the dip aside to cool a little.

Rinse the prawns and pat dry. Thread the prawns onto wooden skewers, using three or four on each. Sprinkle with salt. Heat the oil in a frying pan over high heat and sear the prawns, turning them once. The prawns should still be a little glassy in the middle. Drizzle the prawns with lemon juice and serve with the dip and sliced baguette.

Makes 6–8 skewers

800 g (1 lb 12 oz) raw prawns, peeled and deveined
Salt
4 tbsp canola oil
Juice of ½ lemon

For the dip:
1 celery stalk
2 large garlic cloves
1 tbsp canola oil
400 g (14 oz) jar tomato passata (puréed tomatoes)
3 tbsp sriracha sauce
1 tbsp honey
1 tsp Worcestershire sauce
Salt
Freshly ground black pepper

Also:
1 crusty baguette, for serving

Macaroni cheese is a popular staple of Canadian cuisine. No wonder, as this cheesy, creamy pasta dish delivers quick and easy comfort food. Feel free to experiment with different types of cheese, although cheeses with a high fat content are ideal, as they melt best.

One-pot mac & cheese

Serves 4

½ bunch chives
1 garlic clove
2 cups (500 ml) milk
2 cups (500 ml) vegetable
  stock
2½ cups (400 g) macaroni
½ cup (50 g) grated parmesan
1 cup (100 g) grated cheddar
1 tsp freshly grated nutmeg
Salt
Freshly ground black pepper

Rinse the chives and shake off excess water. Chop finely and set aside.

Peel and finely mince the garlic clove. Add the milk, stock, garlic and macaroni to a large saucepan and briefly bring to the boil. Reduce the heat to low and simmer, stirring occasionally, for about 20 minutes until the pasta is al dente.

Remove the pan from the heat as soon as the pasta is done and add the grated cheese. Stir gently until the cheese has melted. Season with nutmeg, salt and pepper.

Divide the pasta among four plates and serve garnished with the chopped chives.

This traditional pie with its savoury minced meat filling comes from the French-Canadian province of Quebec. It is commonly served at festive occasions. The filling varies between one region and the next. Some versions of tourtière are made with fish and potatoes.

Tourtière

Preheat the oven to 180°C (350°F). Brush the yufka sheets with olive oil on both sides.

Wash and thinly slice the leek. Coarsely chop the bread roll and soak in the milk. Transfer the beef and pork to a mixing bowl, combine with the egg and season with salt and pepper. Squeeze out the excess milk from the soaked bread. Stir into the beef and pork mixture, along with the sliced leek. Season again with salt and pepper.

Place a yufka sheet into a 24 cm (9½ inch) pie dish or springform tin and spread the filling on top. Top with the remaining pastry sheets, pushing them together into decorative folds. Sprinkle with nigella and caraway seeds and bake for about 35 minutes until cooked through and golden on top.

Makes one 24 cm
(9½ inch) pie

4 sheets yufka or filo pastry
2 tbsp olive oil
100 g (3½ oz) leek
1 stale bread roll
200 ml (7 fl oz) milk
250 g (9 oz) beef mince
250 g (9 oz) pork mince
1 egg
Salt
Freshly ground black pepper

Also:
1 tbsp nigella seeds
1 tbsp caraway seeds

Beavers are Canada's national animal and also feature on Canadian 5-cent coins. Reason enough to dedicate these bite-sized delicacies to beavers! In Canada, these are sometimes also called Beaver Tails because of their shape. They are traditionally turned in cinnamon sugar after deep-frying and served with different toppings.

Beaver bites

Makes 20–30

5 tsp dry yeast
350 ml (12 fl oz) lukewarm
  milk
1 pinch sugar
4 tbsp sugar
1 tsp ground cinnamon
1½ tsp salt
2 eggs
4 tbsp canola oil
4 cups (600 g) plain flour,
  plus extra for dusting

For the topping:
1 tbsp canola oil
⅔ cup (200 g) chocolate
  hazelnut spread
Icing (confectioners') sugar,
  for dusting

Also:
8 cups (2 litres) peanut oil,
  for deep-frying

Combine the dry yeast, milk and a pinch of sugar in a mixing bowl. Set aside at room temperature for 15 minutes. Add the remaining ingredients and knead the dough in a food processor for 6 minutes. Place a small heatproof bowl of boiling water in the oven. Cover the dough with a tea towel and place it inside the oven. Leave to rise for 2 hours with the oven door closed.

Remove the dough from the bowl and knead briefly on a lightly floured surface. Roll out the dough to about 1 cm (½ inch) thick and cut out rounds with a 5 cm (2 inch) cookie cutter. Leave the dough rounds to rest for 10 minutes.

Pour the peanut oil into a large saucepan and heat to 180°C (350°F). Deep-fry the dough rounds in batches until golden brown. Transfer the beaver bites onto paper towel to drain off excess oil.

For the topping, whisk the oil into the chocolate hazelnut spread and heat the mixture in the microwave until it is liquid. Serve the beaver bites dusted with icing sugar and drizzled with the chocolate hazelnut spread.

If you ask Canadians about their favourite dessert, these little tarts with their irresistibly creamy filling will probably rank somewhere at the top. The traditional recipe can vary widely between one family and the next, with some adding raisins, pecans or walnuts to the filling.

Butter tarts

For the dough, finely dice the butter. Transfer the flour and diced butter to a mixing bowl and rub together with your fingers until the mixture resembles coarse breadcrumbs. Add the water, egg yolk and vinegar and knead until the dough just comes together in a ball. Wrap in plastic wrap and refrigerate for 2 hours.

For the filling, whisk the butter, muscovado sugar, vanilla sugar and salt until light and creamy. Add the egg and stir until the mixture is well combined.

Preheat the oven to 200°C (400°F). Grease a 12-hole muffin tin and line a baking tray with baking paper. Roll out two-thirds of the dough on a lightly floured surface until about 1 cm (½ inch) thick. Use an 8 cm (3¼ inch) cookie cutter to cut out 12 circles. Transfer the circles to the muffin tin. Divide the filling among the bases. Roll out the remaining dough and use a cookie cutter or small sharp knife to cut out 12 leaves. Place the leaves on the baking tray. Bake the tarts and pastry leaves on the middle rack of the oven for 15 minutes or until the edges turn golden brown.

Set the tarts and leaves aside to cool for 10 minutes. Slide the handle of a teaspoon around the edges of the tarts to release from the tin. Top each tart with a pastry leaf. Leave to cool completely. These are best eaten on the day they're made.

Makes 12

For the dough:
½ cup (125 g) cold butter
1½ cups (220 g) plain flour, plus extra for dusting
¼ cup (60 ml) iced water
1 large egg yolk
1 tsp apple cider vinegar

For the filling:
¼ cup (60 g) butter, softened, plus extra for greasing
200 g (7 oz) muscovado sugar
1½ tbsp vanilla sugar
1 pinch salt
1 large egg

IN CANADA

Charles Dickens

We left Kingston for Montreal on the tenth of May, at half-past nine in the morning, and proceeded in a steamboat down the St. Lawrence river. The beauty of this noble stream at almost any point, but especially in the commencement of this journey when it winds its way among the thousand Islands, can hardly be imagined. The number and constant successions of these islands, all green and richly wooded; their fluctuating sizes, some so large that for half an hour together one among them will appear as the opposite bank of the river, and some so small that they are mere dimples on its broad bosom; their infinite variety of shapes; and the numberless combinations of beautiful forms which the trees growing on them present: all form a picture fraught with uncommon interest and pleasure.

In the afternoon we shot down some rapids where the river boiled and bubbled strangely, and where the force and headlong violence of the current were tremendous. At seven o'clock we reached Dickenson's Landing, whence travellers proceed for two or three hours by stage-coach: the navigation of the river being rendered so dangerous and difficult in the interval, by rapids, that steamboats do not make the passage. The number and length of those *portages*, over which the roads are bad, and the travelling slow, render the way between the towns of Montreal and Kingston, somewhat tedious.

Our course lay over a wide, unenclosed tract of country at a little distance from the river-side, whence the bright warning lights on the dangerous parts of the St. Lawrence shone vividly. The night was dark and raw, and the way dreary enough. It was nearly ten o'clock when we reached the wharf where the next steamboat lay; and went on board, and to bed.

She lay there all night, and started as soon as it was day. The morning was ushered in by a violent thunderstorm, and was very wet, but gradually improved and brightened up. Going on deck after breakfast, I was amazed to see floating down with the stream, a most gigantic raft, with some thirty or forty wooden houses upon it, and at least as many flag-masts, so that it looked like a nautical street. I saw many of these rafts afterwards, but never one so large. All the timber, or 'lumber', as it is called in America, which is brought down the St. Lawrence, is floated down in this manner. When the raft reaches its place of destination, it is broken up; the materials are sold; and the boatmen return for more. ❧

There's no dessert that's more typically Canadian than Nanaimo bars, which are named after the Canadian city of Nanaimo. With three layers consisting of a biscuit crumble and nut base, a cream filling and chocolate topping, they are a little like a layered custard cake but require no baking.

Nanaimo bars

Makes about 24 pieces

For the base:
½ cup (125 g) butter, plus extra for greasing
120 g (4¼ oz) dark chocolate
3 tbsp brown sugar
2 tbsp raw cocoa powder
120 g (4¼ oz) digestive biscuits
1 cup (120 g) walnuts
½ cup (50 g) desiccated coconut

For the filling:
700 ml (24 fl oz) full-cream milk
1 vanilla bean
50 g (1¾ oz) cornflour
100 g (3½ oz) sugar
2 eggs
2 egg yolks
1 cup (250 g) butter, softened

For the topping:
100 g (3½ oz) milk chocolate
100 g (3½ oz) dark chocolate
2 tbsp canola oil
4 tbsp desiccated coconut, for sprinkling

Butter a 22 cm (8½ inch) square cake tin and line with baking paper. For the base, grate the chocolate and transfer to a small saucepan along with the butter, brown sugar and cocoa. Gently heat to melt, stirring continuously.

Place the biscuits inside a resealable plastic bag and pound them to fine crumbs with a rolling pin. Chop the walnuts. Thoroughly combine the chocolate mixture, biscuit crumbs, chopped walnuts and coconut in a large mixing bowl. Transfer the mixture to the cake tin. Press down firmly with your hands and refrigerate for 30 minutes.

For the filling, heat the milk in a saucepan. Split the vanilla bean lengthwise and scrape out the seeds. Add to the milk. Stir briefly and set aside for 15 minutes to infuse with the flavour. Whisk the cornflour, sugar, eggs and egg yolks together in a large bowl. Bring the milk to the boil briefly. Add about 100 ml (3½ fl oz) of the hot milk to the egg mixture and whisk to combine.

Pour the egg mixture into the hot milk, stirring continuously for another 2 minutes. Remove the pan from the heat and leave the custard to cool. Beat the butter until light and creamy, then gradually whisk into the cooled custard. Spread the custard evenly over the chocolate base and refrigerate for 2 hours.

For the topping, finely chop the milk and dark chocolate. Melt in the microwave together with the canola oil. Quickly spread the topping over the chilled custard layer and sprinkle with coconut. Refrigerate for at least 6 hours. Lift out of the tin with the baking paper and cut into small pieces to serve.

Go your own way

On the road! We are totally in tune with our own rhythm of movement and rest. Everyday life in the city seems a million miles away. We live in the moment. Our needs are pared back to the minimum, and we rest much more within ourselves. Our senses seem heightened, and we immerse ourselves in breathtaking views, cool breezes, the scent of the forest...

You'll never know until you go.

Lobster roll

For the brioche dough, peel and quarter the potatoes and cook in salted water until soft. Drain and set aside for 10 minutes to cool. Transfer the remaining ingredients for the dough, except the butter, to a large mixing bowl. Add the potatoes and combine to make a smooth dough, kneading for about 5 minutes by hand or using the dough hook of an electric mixer. Add one-third of the butter and continue kneading to incorporate. Repeat with the remaining butter and knead for another 5 minutes.

Cover the dough with a clean tea towel and leave to rise in a warm spot for about 1 hour. Once it has doubled in volume, remove the dough from the bowl and knead briefly on a lightly floured surface. Divide the dough into 8 portions and shape each portion into a ball. Shape the balls into oblong rolls on a floured surface, applying gentle pressure. Line a baking tray with baking paper and transfer the rolls to the tray, keeping them at least 5 cm (2 inches) apart.

Place the tray in the oven and place a small bowl of boiling water underneath it. Keep the oven door closed and leave the dough to prove for another hour. Once it has again doubled in volume, remove the tray and preheat the oven to 200°C (400°F). Whisk the egg with 1 tablespoon water. Brush the rolls evenly with the mixture and bake until golden brown, about 15 minutes. Remove from the oven and cover with a clean, damp tea towel.

For the filling, place the butter in a small saucepan and brown lightly over medium heat. Finely chop the lobster and parsley and add to the browned butter along with the lemon juice. Briefly toss the lobster in the butter. Remove from the heat. Season with salt and pepper.

Slice the cooled rolls open lengthwise. Divide the filling among the rolls and serve with home-made mayonnaise.

Makes 8 rolls

For the potato brioche dough:
100 g (3½ oz) floury potatoes
Salt
40 g (1½ oz) fresh yeast or
   20 g (¾ oz) dry yeast
150 ml (5 fl oz) lukewarm milk
2⅓ cups (350 g) strong bread
   flour, plus extra for dusting
2 tbsp brown sugar
1 tsp salt
1 egg yolk
45 g (1½ oz) butter, softened

For the filling:
50 g (1¾ oz) butter
600 g (1 lb 5 oz) cooked lobster,
   peeled
4 sprigs flat-leaf parsley
Juice of ½ lemon
Salt
Freshly ground black pepper

Also:
1 egg, lightly beaten, for brushing
Mayonnaise (see p. 114),
   for serving

In many countries, chips are eaten with tomato sauce or vinegar. Try a different, authentically Canadian version of everyone's favourite fast food with gravy and haloumi cheese. You'll be hooked in no time!

Poutine

Serves 4

For the gravy:
500 g (1 lb 2 oz) soup
  vegetables (carrot, onion,
  celeriac, leek)
1 garlic bulb
500 g (1 lb 2 oz) beef bones
  or 4 cups (1 litre) beef stock
2 tbsp tomato paste
  (concentrated purée)
1 tbsp canola oil
2 bay leaves
4 juniper berries
3–5 tbsp cornflour

For the chips:
1 kg (2 lb 4 oz) floury
  potatoes
1 tbsp plain flour
8 cups (2 litres) canola oil

For the topping:
225 g (8 oz) haloumi
2 sprigs flat-leaf parsley

Preheat the oven to 200°C (400°F). For the gravy, wash and coarsely dice the soup vegetables. Place the vegetables, garlic and beef bones on a baking tray and roast for 30 minutes.

Heat the tomato paste and canola oil in a large saucepan. Deglaze with a little water. Transfer the roast vegetables, beef bones, bay leaves and juniper berries to the saucepan and add 8 cups (2 litres) water. Simmer for 2 hours to reduce the liquid by half. (If using beef stock, simply pour over the roast vegetables –you won't need the beef bones in this case.)

Strain the liquid into another saucepan through a fine sieve. Bring to the boil. Dissolve the cornflour in 3 tablespoons cold water and slowly whisk into the gravy until it reaches the desired consistency. Set aside.

Thoroughly wash the potatoes and cut them into chips. Transfer to a bowl and toss with the flour. Heat the oil to 180°C (350°F) in a large saucepan. Deep-fry the chips in two batches, stirring occasionally. Cook until golden brown, remove with a slotted spoon and drain on paper towel.

Divide the chips among serving plates and crumble the haloumi over the top. Pour the warm gravy over the chips and serve immediately, garnished with a little parsley.

In Canada, fishing for halibut is a centuries-old tradition. Halibut is renowned for its firm, sweet flesh. It can be cooked fresh, but also dried or smoked. Served with bacon inside squid ink buns, it makes a burger that tastes as extraordinary as it looks.

Ink-black halibut burgers

Prepare the potato brioche dough. Once it has proven, knead in a few drops of squid ink paste until the dough turns completely black. Divide the dough into 8 portions and shape each into a bun. Transfer the buns to a baking tray lined with baking paper, cover with a tea towel and leave to rise for 1 hour. Preheat the oven to 200°C (400°F) and bake the buns for about 15 minutes. Remove from the oven and cover with a clean, damp tea towel.

For the dressing, peel the shallot and chop very finely together with the capers. Combine with the mayonnaise and season with lemon juice.

Divide the halibut fillet into 8 even portions. Heat a frying pan over medium heat. Add the halibut and bacon strips and fry until the bacon has browned. Carefully turn the fillets once and season with salt.

Remove the fish and bacon from the pan. Split the buns and toast them in the pan, cut side down. Separate the lettuce leaves, wash and spin dry. Spread the bottom bun halves with the dressing and top with a few lettuce leaves. Add a piece of fish and two strips of bacon to each bun and top with the remaining bun halves.

Makes 8 burgers

For the buns:
Potato brioche dough
   (see p. 97)
A few drops of squid
   ink paste

For the dressing:
1 French shallot
4 capers
1 quantity mayonnaise
   (see p. 114)
Juice of ½ lemon

Also:
500 g (1 lb 2 oz) halibut or
   other firm white fish fillet
16 strips bacon
Salt
1 head lettuce

Clam chowder

Serves 4

500 g (1 lb 2 oz) floury
   potatoes
500 g (1 lb 2 oz) mussels
   or clams
2 cups (500 ml) fish stock
2 corn cobs
2 French shallots
1 bunch flat-leaf parsley
2 tbsp butter
4 tbsp plain flour
2 cups (500 ml) cream
Salt
Freshly ground black pepper

Peel and finely dice the potatoes. Wash the mussels or clams very thoroughly. Pour the fish stock into a saucepan. Add the potatoes, bring to a simmer and cook until almost done.

Wash the corn cobs and cut off the kernels with a sharp knife. Add the corn kernels to the stock. Cook until the potatoes are tender, then remove from the heat.

Peel and finely dice the shallots. Rinse the parsley, shake off excess water and finely chop the leaves. Sweat the shallots with the butter in a large saucepan over medium heat. Add the flour and sweat for 1 minute, stirring. Deglaze the roux with the cream and bring to the boil.

Finally, add the fish stock mixture, along with the mussels or clams and parsley and cook until the shells open (discard any that don't open). Continue to simmer for another 2 minutes, season with salt and pepper and divide among four bowls.

Many dishes in Canadian cooking, including this one, can be traced back to France or are very much inspired by French cuisine. Clam chowder is a very smooth, creamy clam soup that has become very popular all over the world. If you like, you can substitute white wine for some of the stock.

Risotto is an Italian classic that is loved all over the world for its creaminess and versatility. Canadians, who love fish and seafood, have developed their own version of seafood risotto prepared with fish stock. Served with fennel and prawns, this makes for a uniquely tasty dish.

Seafood risotto

Peel and finely dice the shallots. Remove the tough core from the fennel and slice into thin strips. Set the fennel fronds aside for garnish. Sweat the shallots in the olive oil in a saucepan. Add the risotto rice and continue to sweat briefly. Pour in the white wine and stir until the rice has absorbed the liquid.

Meanwhile, bring the fish stock to the boil in a separate saucepan. Wash the mussels or clams thoroughly and add them to the fish stock. Remove them from the stock once the shells have opened. Set aside and keep warm.

Add the fish stock to the risotto, one ladleful at a time, and allow the rice to absorb all of the liquid before adding more. Keep adding stock until you have a creamy risotto and the rice is cooked with a tiny little bite.

Rinse the fish, pat dry and cut into bite-sized pieces. Once the risotto has the desired consistency, stir in the parmesan and butter. At the same time, heat the canola oil in a frying pan. Pat the prawns dry and add to the pan along with the fish and sear over high heat. Divide the risotto among bowls, arrange the fish, prawns and mussels or clams on top and serve garnished with fennel fronds.

Serves 4

2 French shallots
½ bulb fennel
2 tbsp olive oil
240 g (7¾ oz) risotto rice
1 cup (250 ml) white wine
About 400 ml (14 fl oz)
    fish stock
200 g (7 oz) mussels or clams
400 g (14 oz) fish (e.g. cod)
⅔ cup (60 g) grated
    parmesan
1 tbsp cold butter
2 tbsp canola oil
200 g (7 oz) prawns, peeled
    and deveined

FOR ONE MINUTE DON'T TALK,
DON'T READ, NO PHOTOS.
JUST LOOK AND SEE...

Savoury pies are incredibly popular all over Canada. In this recipe, flaky puff pastry encloses chicken and mushrooms, but feel free to give your imagination free rein in developing your own fillings. Leftover Sunday roast chicken or lamb is a delicious choice, for example.

Chicken and mushroom pot pie

Serves 4–6

100 g (3½ oz) spring onions
   (scallions)
500 g (1 lb 2 oz) mixed
   mushrooms (chanterelles,
   button mushrooms, oyster
   mushrooms)
300 g (10½ oz) chicken
   breast fillet
3 tbsp canola oil
1 sheet frozen puff pastry
1½ tbsp cornflour
1 tsp mustard
2 tbsp crème fraîche
200 ml (7 fl oz) chicken stock
Salt
Pepper

Also:
1 egg, lightly beaten,
   for brushing

Wash, trim and thinly slice the spring onions. Set aside a little for garnish. Wipe the mushrooms with a clean tea towel and coarsely dice. Pat the chicken dry and slice into thin strips. Heat the canola oil in a frying pan over high heat. Add the mushrooms and sear until golden brown. Add the chicken strips and spring onions and continue to fry briefly.

Remove the puff pastry from the freezer and leave to soften a little. Combine the cornflour, mustard, crème fraîche, chicken stock, salt and pepper until the cornflour has dissolved. Add the mixture to the chicken and mushrooms, stirring continuously, and briefly bring everything to the boil. Pour the mixture into a 25 x 15 cm (10 x 6 inch) baking tin.

Preheat the oven to 180°C (350°F). Cut the puff pastry sheet to fit the baking tin. Carefully place the pastry over the filling and press the edges to stick to the tin. Generously brush the beaten egg all over the pastry. Cut a cross into the centre of the pie to allow the steam to escape as it cooks. Bake until golden brown, about 30 minutes.

Harvesting molluscs has a long tradition all along Canada's coastline. Canadian scallops are highly sought-after for their unique flavour and texture, which are given more time to develop in the country's cold waters than elsewhere. Cooked over a barbecue, they are particularly tender.

Pear salad with grilled scallops

For the dressing, rinse the lemon thyme and shake off excess water. Pick off the leaves and transfer to a tall beaker together with the other ingredients. Briefly blend with a stick blender.

Wash and pick through the lamb's lettuce. Spin dry and transfer to a large salad bowl. Quarter the pears and remove the cores. Slice lengthwise into thin wedges. Dry-roast the pine nuts in a frying pan until golden brown.

Rinse the scallops and pat dry. Remove the muscle on the side, if it is still attached. Heat your barbecue or a chargrill pan. Sear the scallops on the very hot barbecue or pan for about 1 minute on each side.

Pour the dressing over the lettuce and toss gently to combine. Top with the pear wedges and pine nuts. Place the hot scallops on top and serve immediately.

Serves 4

400 g (14 oz) lamb's lettuce
2 ripe pears
4 tbsp pine nuts
12 scallops

For the dressing:
2 sprigs lemon thyme
1½ tbsp honey
Juice of 1 lemon
100 ml (3½ fl oz) canola oil
Salt
Freshly ground black pepper

Mayonnaise isn't difficult to make at home, and you'll probably have everything you need in your kitchen. The little effort it takes really pays off – you'll always taste the difference between shop-bought and fresh mayonnaise.

Mayonnaise

Makes 150 g (5½ oz)

1 fresh egg
1 tbsp dijon mustard
½ cup (125 ml) canola oil
25 ml (¾ fl oz) olive oil
1 tbsp apple cider vinegar
Salt
Freshly ground black pepper

Crack the egg and transfer it to a tall beaker. Add the mustard and oils. Place the blades of a stick blender directly onto the egg yolk and mustard. Switch the blender on at medium speed and very slowly pull it upwards to make a thick, creamy mayonnaise. Season with cider vinegar, salt and pepper.

This barbecue sauce is the perfect accompaniment to so many dishes and occasions that it is best prepared in large quantities. It's incredibly quick and easy to make and so delicious that you'll probably never want to buy bottled barbecue sauce again.

Barbecue sauce

Add the passata, tomato paste, mustard, jam, honey, curry powder and apple juice to a small saucepan. Bring to the boil. Simmer over medium heat for about 15 minutes. Season the sauce with salt and chilli flakes and transfer into a jar while still hot.

Makes 1 jar

250 g (9 oz) jar tomato
   passata (puréed tomatoes)
1 tbsp tomato paste
   (concentrated purée)
1 tbsp sweet mustard
1 tbsp blackcurrant jam
2 tsp honey
1 tsp hot curry powder
2½ tbsp apple juice
Salt
Chilli flakes, to taste

Only travel can tame my wild heart.

No Canadian cookbook would be complete without a smoked fish recipe. Smoking is a traditional cooking technique that not only preserves the fish, but also imparts a unique flavour. This recipe takes a little longer to prepare for marinating and smoking the fish, but it is still very easy to make. The trout goes perfectly with fresh bread and potato salad (see p.60).

Smoked trout

Rinse the trout and pine needles and place in a large roasting tin. Whisk the water and salt until the salt has completely dissolved. Pour the salt water over the trout, cover the tin with plastic wrap and refrigerate overnight.

Fire up your barbecue the next day. Combine the smoking chips and apple juice and set aside for 15 minutes to infuse. Push the coals to the side as soon as they glow white.

Remove the fish and pine needles from the brine, rinse thoroughly and dry thoroughly with paper towel. Wash the lemons under hot water, pat dry and slice. Rinse the rosemary and shake dry. Stuff the trout with the sliced lemon and rosemary. Tie the fish with kitchen twine to secure the aromatics inside.

Drain the smoking chips well and place them on the hot coals along with the pine needles. Immediately place the trout on the barbecue grill and close the lid. The temperature inside should be about 60–80°C (140–175°F). Cook the fish for 45 minutes before removing them from the barbecue. Best served warm.

Makes 4 trout

4 kitchen-ready trout, about
 250 g (9 oz) each
1 handful fresh pine needles
8 cups (2 litres) lukewarm
 water
1 tbsp salt
2 lemons
2 sprigs rosemary

Also:
1 handful smoking chips
200 ml (7 fl oz) apple juice

Chocolate tastes great in many guises, but what could be better than a delectably moist chocolate pudding cake? Eat this as comfort food, to celebrate an occasion, with good friends or just because – it will always delight. It's best served warm with vanilla ice cream.

Chocolate pudding cake

Serves 4

150 g (5½ oz) dark chocolate
   (min. 70%)
75 g (2½ oz) butter
150 g (5½ oz) sugar
3 eggs

Also:
Icing (confectioners') sugar,
   for dusting

Preheat the oven to 180°C (350°F). Coarsely chop the chocolate and finely dice the butter. Transfer the chocolate, butter and sugar to a heatproof bowl. Place the bowl over a saucepan of simmering water to melt, stirring continuously. Remove the saucepan from the heat and leave the chocolate mixture to cool a little.

Briefly whisk the eggs and stir into the chocolate mixture. Divide the mixture among four ramekins or ovenproof mugs and bake for about 25 minutes. Remove from the oven, dust with icing sugar and serve warm.

Soft, warm cinnamon scrolls with sweet icing are a real treat that can be made even better by adding a little bacon. Canadian bacon is relatively low in fat, which gives it a slightly sweet flavour and makes it perfect for sweet as well as savoury dishes. If that's too much of a culinary adventure for you, these cinnamon scrolls are also fabulous without bacon!

Cinnamon scrolls with bacon

Transfer all of the yeast dough ingredients to a large mixing bowl. Process with the dough hook of an electric mixer for 6–8 minutes to make a smooth dough. Shape the dough into a ball, cover and leave to rise for 1 hour in the bowl until it has doubled in volume.

For the filling, combine the butter with the cinnamon, cardamom and icing sugar. Butter a springform tin or square baking tin.

Roll out the dough on a lightly floured surface to make a rectangle 1 cm (½ inch) thick. Spread evenly with the filling and roll up tightly from one of the long sides. Cut the dough into 5 cm (2 inch) slices and transfer these onto the baking tray, keeping them about 3 cm (1¼ inches) apart. Cover and leave to rise in a warm place for 30 minutes.

Preheat the oven to 200°C (400°F). Transfer the baking tray to the oven. Bake the scrolls for about 17 minutes. Set aside to cool a little.

For the icing, combine 1 tablespoon water with the icing sugar. Add a little more water, if necessary, until the icing has the desired consistency. Drizzle the icing over the warm scrolls. Heat a frying pan over medium heat and fry the bacon until crisp. Dice finely and sprinkle over the scrolls.

TIP This dough also makes great bread for French toast. Simply leave to rise in the bowl as described above, knead again briefly to deflate and then shape into a loaf. Transfer to a loaf tin lined with baking paper and leave to rise for 30 minutes. Bake in the preheated oven at 200 °C (400°F) for 20 minutes.

Makes about 9

For the yeast dough:
10 g (¼ oz) egg yolk
1⅔ cups (250 g) strong bread
   flour, plus extra for dusting
½ cup (125 ml) lukewarm milk
1½ tbsp sugar
1 tbsp butter, softened, plus
   extra for greasing
10 g (¼ oz) lard
1 pinch salt
21 g (¾ oz) fresh yeast
Seeds of 1 vanilla bean
Grated zest of ½ lemon

For the filling:
80 g (2¾ oz) butter, melted
2 tbsp ground cinnamon
½ tsp ground cardamom
3 tbsp icing (confectioners')
   sugar

For the icing:
100 g (3½ oz) icing
   (confectioners') sugar

Also:
100 g (3½ oz) bacon

Iced tea is a fabulous drink, not only on hot summer days. Combined with fresh cranberries and rosemary, it makes a refreshing punch with a unique aroma.

Home-made iced tea with cranberries

Makes about 1.4 litres (49 fl oz)

3 tbsp raw sugar
Seeds of 1 vanilla bean
1 sprig rosemary
3 fruit infusion tea bags
2 cups (200 g) cranberries
400 ml (14 fl oz) cranberry juice
Ice cubes

Bring 4 cups (1 litre) water to the boil in a saucepan with the raw sugar, vanilla seeds and rosemary. Immerse the tea bags in the hot water and leave to infuse for 5 minutes. Squeeze out and remove.

Add the cranberries to the pan and gently crush with a potato masher to release some of their juice. Set the tea aside until completely cooled.

Add the cranberry juice and ice cubes to the cooled tea, stir and serve immediately.

Canadian blueberries are sold both wild and commercially grown. During their season, which lasts from early July to late August, they are initially harvested by hand and only later by machine. Sweet blueberries are perfect for any number of dishes, from cakes through to muffins and pancakes, but they are also great in some savoury combinations.

Toasted crostini with blueberries

Preheat the oven to 200°C (400°F). Spread the blueberries on a baking tray lined with baking paper. Drizzle with 2 tablespoons of the lemon juice and the honey. Transfer the tray to the oven and roast the berries until soft but still intact, about 7–10 minutes. Remove and set aside to cool.

Preheat the oven using the grill function. Rub the baguette slices with the halved garlic clove. Transfer to a baking tray lined with baking paper and drizzle with a little olive oil. Toast briefly in the oven until just brown.

Combine the goat's curd with 2 tablespoons of the lemon juice and the lemon zest in a small bowl. Spread the baguette slices with the curd mixture and top with the blueberries. Serve the toasts drizzled with a little honey and garnished with rosemary.

Makes 12

1⅓ cups (200 g) blueberries
Grated zest and juice of
  1 lemon
1 tbsp honey, plus extra
  for drizzling
12 slices baguette
1 garlic clove
Olive oil
250 g (9 oz) goat's curd

Also:
Rosemary, for garnish

FIND WATER
BY FOLLOWING
THE SOUND OF
A FLOWING RIVER

Blissful solitude

The evening holds peace and brings regeneration with a warm fire, a simple shelter, good food and deep rest. Looking into the starry sky above, we are very much aware of our own tiny size and insignificance. Under the vast night sky, we feel every cell of our bodies alive with every breath.

Canada, being a country that welcomes immigration, is a culinary melting pot. Fusing influences of very different national and regional cuisines, new recipes have evolved, including this cauldron goulash, which was originally a traditional – or even national – dish of Hungary. This Canadian version adds British ale for an Anglo touch.

Cauldron goulash with pale ale

Serves 4–6

1 onion
1 large garlic clove
1 carrot
100 g (3½ oz) celeriac
1 kg (2 lb 4 oz) diced beef
Salt
Ground paprika
3 tbsp canola oil
1 tbsp tomato paste
    (concentrated purée)
1 cup (250 ml) pale ale
250 g (9 oz) jar tomato
    passata (puréed tomatoes)
2 juniper berries
1 red capsicum (pepper)
2 tbsp maple syrup
Freshly ground black pepper

Also:
Thyme, for garnish

Peel and finely chop the onion and garlic clove. Peel and finely dice the carrot and celeriac. Pat the beef dry and cut into bite-sized pieces, if necessary. Season the meat with salt and paprika. Place a large roasting tin over high heat, add the oil and beef and sear.

Remove the meat as soon as it has browned all over. Add the onion, garlic, carrot and celeriac to the tin and briefly fry. Stir in the tomato paste and briefly cook. Return the meat to the tin and deglaze everything with the pale ale and passata. Add the juniper berries. Reduce the heat to low and simmer the goulash for about 2 hours until the meat is tender but does not fall apart.

Meanwhile, wash the capsicum and cut into thin strips, removing the seeds and any white membrane. Add to the goulash 15 minutes before the meat is done. Season the goulash with maple syrup, salt and pepper before serving and remove the juniper berries. Serve garnished with thyme.

A campfire and damper on a stick bring back so many childhood memories! To prevent the sticks from burning, remove the bark from the tips and soak them in water for some time before wrapping the dough around them.

Onion campfire bread with Cajun spice butter

For the yeast dough, peel and finely dice the onion. Heat a frying pan over medium heat. Add the olive oil and onion and fry until caramelised. Rinse the rosemary and shake off excess water. Pick off the leaves. Chop finely and set aside.

Transfer the dough ingredients to a large mixing bowl and process with the dough hook of an electric mixer to make a smooth dough. Cover with a clean tea towel and set aside for 1 hour.

For the Cajun spice butter, peel and finely dice the shallot. Briefly dry-roast in a pan together with the tomato paste. Set aside to cool briefly, then transfer to a small bowl together with the butter. Add the Cajun spice mix and combine well. Refrigerate the butter.

Heat the barbecue or light up a fire pit. Remove small amounts of dough, roll them between your hands and wrap around the sticks in spiral shapes. Cook over the fire and serve with the butter.

TIP You can make this spice mix yourself: combine 2 teaspoons each of black pepper, dried oregano, ground cumin, garlic and onion powder with 1 teaspoon each of dried thyme, ground paprika and cayenne pepper.

Serves 4

For the yeast dough:
1 onion
2 tbsp olive oil
1 sprig rosemary
1 kg (2 lb 4 oz) plain flour
2 cups (500 ml) lukewarm
   water
1 tbsp sugar
2 tbsp salt
40 g (1½ oz) fresh yeast

For the Cajun spice butter:
1 large French shallot
2 tsp tomato paste
   (concentrated purée)
100 g (3½ oz) butter,
   softened
1 tsp Cajun spice mix
   (see Tip)

Also:
4 clean wooden sticks

Whether in hot campfire coals or over a barbecue, baked potatoes are easy to prepare and a true classic of outdoor cooking. If possible, use wild Canadian salmon for this recipe, which is traditionally cured briefly before smoking.

Baked potatoes with herbed sour cream and salmon

Serves 4–6

8 large, floury potatoes
1 tbsp canola oil
½ cup (60 g) salt

For the sour cream:
1 bunch mixed herbs
  (e.g. parsley, dill, chives)
150 g (5½ oz) cream cheese
300 g (10½ oz) thick sour
  cream
Juice of 1 lemon

For the filling:
400 g (14 oz) cured or grilled
  salmon (see p. 158)
1⅔ cups (100 g) alfalfa sprouts

Heat the barbecue with coals or prepare a fire pit. Cut eight pieces of foil for the potatoes. Wash and pat the potatoes dry. Generously rub with the oil and salt. Wrap each potato in foil and place in the white-hot coals.

For the sour cream, rinse the herbs, shake off excess water and chop finely. Combine with the remaining ingredients and whisk to make a smooth cream.

Remove the potatoes from the coals after about 45–60 minutes, depending on their size. Open up the foil and slice the potatoes open lengthwise. Top with the sour cream, salmon and sprouts.

PULLED PORK BURGERS

For the marinade, chop all of the spices in a small food processor or spice grinder until there are no large pieces left. Rinse the pork neck and pat dry. Rub thoroughly with the marinade. Transfer to a resealable plastic bag or wrap in plastic wrap and refrigerate for 1–3 days to marinate.

For the coleslaw, quarter the cabbage, remove the core and thinly slice using a sharp knife or mandolin. Add the mayonnaise and buttermilk to the cabbage and massage everything together well with your hands. Season with salt and pepper.

Prepare the potato brioche dough according to the recipe. Divide the dough into eight portions after proving and shape each portion into a bun. Transfer the buns to a baking tray lined with baking paper, cover with a tea towel and leave to rise for 1 hour. Preheat the oven to 180°C (350°F). Brush the buns with egg yolk and bake for 20 minutes. Remove from the oven and cover with a clean, damp tea towel.

Combine the smoking chips and apple juice and set aside for about 15 minutes to infuse. Meanwhile, heat your grill. Pat the meat dry. Drain the smoking chips. Once the coals are white hot, push them to the side and cover them with smoking chips. Immediately place the barbecue rack on the grill, add the meat and close the barbecue lid. Smoke the meat for 30 minutes.

Preheat the oven to 120°C (235°F). Generously brush the meat with one-third of the barbecue sauce. Transfer the meat to an oven rack and place inside the oven, with a large roasting tin underneath to catch all the juices. Roast the meat for about 8 hours, brushing it with barbecue sauce every 2 hours, until the core temperature reaches 90°C (195°F). Remove the meat from the oven, cover with foil and set aside to rest for 30 minutes. Transfer the meat to the roasting tin and pull it into bite-sized pieces using two forks. Pour the remaining barbecue sauce over the top and toss to combine.

Halve the buns, top with pulled pork and coleslaw and serve the burgers immediately.

Makes 8

2 kg (4 lb 8 oz) high-quality
  pork neck

For the marinade:
3 heaped tbsp sweet paprika
2 heaped tbsp hot paprika
2 tbsp coriander seeds
3 juniper berries
1 bay leaf
2 garlic cloves
2 tbsp salt
3 tbsp sugar
1 tbsp black peppercorns
1 tbsp curry powder

For the coleslaw:
500 g (1 lb 2 oz) cabbage
1 quantity of mayonnaise
  (see p. 114)
200 ml (7 fl oz) buttermilk
Salt
Freshly ground black pepper

For the buns:
Potato brioche dough
  (see p. 97)
1 egg yolk

Also:
2 handfuls smoking chips
2½ tbsp apple juice
Barbecue sauce (see p. 115),
  for serving

TRACKS TO BE FOLLOWED
TRACKS TO BE FOUND

If preparing a delicious barbecue dish with little effort sounds good to you, corn on the cob is just the thing. Buy fresh cobs with green husks, if you can get them, so you can pull off the husks and plait them together. This makes it easy to turn the cobs on the grill.

Grilled corn with chipotle mayonnaise

Serves 4

8 corn cobs (with husks, if possible)
1 tbsp canola oil
Salt

For the chipotle mayonnaise:
1 French shallot
1 garlic clove
2 dried chillies
2 tbsp olive oil
1 fresh egg
1 tbsp dijon mustard
½ cup (125 ml) canola oil
1 tsp honey
1 tsp lime juice
1 tsp smoked paprika
1 tbsp apple cider vinegar
Salt
Freshly ground black pepper

Also:
1 bunch parsley
Wooden skewers (if using corn cobs without husks)

Peel off the husks and plait them together. Rub the corn with the canola oil and salt.

For the chipotle mayonnaise, peel and finely mince the shallot and garlic clove. Finely chop the chillies. Briefly sweat in 1 tablespoon of the olive oil in a frying pan. Set aside to cool a little.

Place the egg in a tall beaker. Add the mustard, canola oil, honey, lime juice, paprika, remaining olive oil and the shallot mixture. Place the blades of a stick blender directly onto the egg yolk. Switch the blender on at medium speed and very slowly pull it upwards to make a thick, creamy mayonnaise. Season with cider vinegar, salt and pepper. Refrigerate.

Rinse the parsley, shake off excess water and pick off the leaves. Grill the corn cobs in a chargrill pan over medium heat or on a preheated barbecue, turning until cooked on all sides. If using husked cobs, cut them into two halves and pierce with a wooden skewer each for turning. Remove the cobs from the pan or grill once they are nicely browned all over. Serve with the chipotle mayonnaise and parsley.

Vegetables make for a lot of variety on the barbecue, in addition to fish and meat. Feel free to experiment with different vegetables, but keep in mind that cooking times will vary.

Warm grilled vegetable salad

Preheat your barbecue. Wash the zucchini, capsicum and beans. Trim the ends off the zucchini, beans and onions. Slice the zucchini lengthwise into thin strips. Peel and quarter the onions. Slice the capsicum lengthwise into thin strips, removing the seeds and any white membrane.

Blanch the beans in boiling salted water for 5 minutes. Drain well. Transfer the vegetables to a bowl and toss with the canola oil.

Rinse the herbs for the herb oil and shake off excess water. Pick off the leaves and chop finely. Combine with the olive oil and season with salt and pepper.

Transfer the vegetables onto the preheated barbecue and grill until just tender. Transfer to a large bowl and combine with the herb oil.

TIP This salad tastes best when served lukewarm, alongside some crusty baguette or campfire bread (see p. 137).

Serves 4

2 zucchini (courgettes)
1 yellow capsicum (pepper)
400 g (14 oz) green beans
3 red onions
2 tbsp canola oil

For the herb oil:
2 sprigs basil
2 sprigs summer savoury
 or thyme
1 sprig rosemary
2 tbsp olive oil
Salt
Freshly ground black pepper

Maple syrup is as quintessentially Canadian as mountains, lakes and ice hockey. When buying maple syrup, check whether it is pure or has other ingredients added. Natural maple syrup is made out of the sap of sugar maple trees, which is reduced to make a sweet syrup. The lighter the colour, the earlier the sap was harvested and the higher the syrup quality.

Maple-glazed spare ribs

Serves 4–6

3 kg (6 lb 12 oz) spare ribs

For the stock:
200 ml (7 fl oz) apple juice
2 bay leaves
2 onions
4 juniper berries
1 garlic bulb
Salt
Freshly ground black pepper

Also:
100 ml (3½ fl oz) maple
    syrup, for brushing

Remove the silver skin from around the ribs. To do so, carefully insert the end of a spoon between the meat and skin and pull the spoon to the left or right. Alternatively, use a sharp carving knife.

Combine all of the stock ingredients in a large saucepan and add the ribs. Pour in enough water to cover the ribs. Bring to the boil, reduce the heat to low and simmer for 2 hours.

Just before the end of the cooking time, preheat the oven to 200°C (400°F) and switch on the grill. Remove the ribs from the stock, drain briefly and transfer to a baking tray, flesh side up. Generously brush with the maple syrup and grill on the top shelf until golden brown, about 5 minutes.

Canadian whisky was long considered to be an insiders' tip for connoisseurs. Scottish and Irish immigrants brought the art of distilling whisky to Canada, which these days produces about 500 whiskies renowned for their outstanding purity. The combination of whisky and smoked paprika turns this chicken into a sensation: juicy, tender and full of flavour.

Whisky roast chicken

Preheat the oven to 130°C (250°F) fan-forced. Rinse the chicken and pat dry. Transfer to a large roasting tin. Combine the whisky with half the canola oil, the smoked paprika and harissa. Season generously with salt.

Peel and quarter the onions. Toss with the remaining canola oil in a small bowl. Add the onions to the roasting tin and pour in 100 ml (3½ fl oz) water.

Rub the chicken with half the marinade. Place in the roasting tin on top of the onions. Roast for 1 hour, then brush with the remaining marinade. Return to the oven to roast for another 1 hour. Cover the dish with foil, if necessary, to prevent the chicken skin from burning.

Remove the roasting tin from the oven. Place the chicken on an oven rack, with the roasting tin underneath to catch the juices. Increase the oven to 200°C (400°F) and roast the chicken for another 20–25 minutes. Serve with bread.

Serves 4–6

1 whole chicken, about 2.5 kg
  (5 lb 8 oz)
2 cups (500 ml) whisky
4 tbsp canola oil
3 tsp smoked paprika
1 tbsp harissa
Salt
5 red onions

**JOBS FILL
YOUR POCKETS
ADVENTURES FILL
YOUR SOUL**

Canadians know how to prepare salmon in any number of ways – after all, the country produces some of the world's best! Grilling salmon fillets on cedarwood planks is especially popular. This method produces a particularly tender fish with an intense aroma. Make sure you use only cedar planks from untreated wood.

Cedar plank salmon fillet

Serves 4

For the pickled onions:
5 large red onions
1 cup (250 ml) red wine
   vinegar
Juice of 1 lime
2 tbsp non-iodised salt
1 tsp sugar
1 bay leaf
Black peppercorns

For the salmon:
1 bunch coriander (cilantro)
1 kg (2 lb 4 oz) salmon fillet,
   skin on
Coarse sea salt

Also:
1 cedarwood plank
   (or beech wood)

Soak the cedar plank in plenty of water overnight.

For the pickled onions, peel the onions and slice into thin rings. Place in a saucepan with the red wine vinegar, lime juice, salt, sugar, bay leaf, peppercorns and 2 cups (500 ml) water. Simmer until the onions just have a little bite. Transfer to pickling jars while still hot.

Preheat a barbecue grill. Rinse the coriander and shake off excess water. Pick off the leaves and set aside. Rinse the salmon and pat dry. Sprinkle with sea salt and place on the cedar plank. Place the plank on the hot grill for 25–30 minutes.

Serve the cooked salmon topped with the pickled onions and garnished with coriander.

This is the North American version of a Sunday roast. The steaks are easy to prepare, and the potatoes don't take much time either, making this the perfect dish to come home to after a day filled with adventures.

Roast beef with smashed potatoes

Preheat the oven to 200°C (400°F). Peel the potatoes and boil them in salted water for 15 minutes.

Halve the garlic bulbs lengthwise and transfer them to a roasting tin with the olive oil. Pat the potatoes dry, add to the garlic and toss to coat with the oil. Bake for 45 minutes. Turn the garlic and gently crush the potatoes with a potato masher. Dot with the butter and continue to bake for another 15 minutes.

Meanwhile, pat the beef dry and remove any tendons. Cut into 2 cm (¾ inch) slices and season with salt and pepper. Heat the olive oil in a frying pan over medium heat. Add the rosemary and sear the steaks for 2–3 minutes on each side. Remove from the pan, wrap in foil and set aside to rest for 10 minutes.

Serve the steaks with the potatoes and the Cajun spice butter or Herbed sour cream.

Serves 4

For the smashed potatoes:
1 kg (2 lb 4 oz) small, floury
    potatoes
Salt
2 garlic bulbs
100 ml (3½ fl oz) olive oil
3 tbsp butter

For the roast beef:
1.5 kg (3 lb 5 oz) piece beef
    fillet, at room temperature
Salt
Pepper
2 tbsp olive oil
1 sprig rosemary

Also:
Cajun spice butter (see p. 137)
    or Herbed sour cream
    (see p. 138), for serving

S'MORES

Combine the flours, bicarbonate of soda, brown sugar, salt, honey, milk, vanilla and cinnamon in a large mixing bowl. Add the butter and knead everything briefly to make a smooth dough.

Preheat the oven to 180°C (350°F). Divide the dough in half and transfer one half onto a sheet of baking paper. Cover with another sheet of baking paper and roll the dough out very thinly to the size of a baking tray. (If you like, spray the paper with a little water underneath to stop it from sliding.) Transfer the dough onto a baking tray and carefully pull off the top sheet of baking paper. Trim to make a rectangle with straight edges, then use a sharp knife to cut the dough into small rectangles. (Otherwise there's a risk that it may break after baking.) Repeat with the remaining dough. Prick the dough all over with a fork.

Bake each tray for 10–15 minutes until the dough has just a little softness left. Remove from the oven and leave to cool completely before breaking the crackers into pieces along the cut marks.

For the s'mores, toast the marshmallows over an open fire until caramelised. Place a hot marshmallow on a cracker, top with a thin piece of chocolate and sandwich together with another cracker.

Makes about 30

For the crackers:
⅔ cup (100 g) plain flour
1⅓ cups (200 g) wholemeal
    plain flour
1 tsp bicarbonate of soda
    (baking soda)
¾ cup (150 g) brown sugar
1 pinch salt
2 tbsp honey
4 tbsp milk
1 tsp vanilla extract
1 tsp ground cinnamon
100 g (3½ oz) butter, melted

Also:
Marshmallows, for serving
Dark chocolate, for serving

ESCAPE AND BREATHE
THE AIR OF NEW PLACES

Cabin
at
Singing
River

Chris Czajkowski

I sit by the singing river and watch the shallow water – quiet and a little drab at this "waiting" time of year – as it slides between mudbanks and sandbars on its uneasy journey down the valley to the sea. It is not always as gentle as this, the river, but the snow and the winter cold still lock the surface water high in the surrounding mountains. Only the sub-terranean currents, which always flow, can seep through rock and glacier-milled gravel to emerge below the tree line and trickle down the steep, green, forested walls of the Atnarko Valley. Upstream from me, a small island, densely covered with birch and winter grey alders, blocks the river and forces it into two complaining strands that run together into deeper water by my feet. On the far bank, three cottonwoods rise from a scribble of under-brush and clasp the hunched shoulders of a mountain, blank with snow, within the frame of their empty arms.

And I wonder, as so many of us do at turning points in our lives, whether I am doing the right thing. I have been offered a chance to build a cabin on this spot, 27 miles from the nearest road and 95 miles from a store, in the heart of

British Columbia's Coast Range. A dream come true is staring me in the face, and I simply don't know if I can handle it.

Oddly enough, my childhood at the edge of a nondescript village in Britain fitted me quite well for the life that I now contemplate. My father was a wartime Polish refugee, and he started a business making furniture and restoring antiques. I played first with the thin, curled shavings swept into aromatic heaps beneath the benches and later with my father's tools. My mother, too, was very creative, and I soon learned that almost anything we wanted could be made.

My parents did not mix socially, and I was a loner. I spent thousands of hours exploring the uninhabited woods and fields behind the house, expeditions that evolved, as my horizons expanded, into two week long solitary hikes in the mountains of New Zealand, in the Andes and on the treeless, roadless, windblown grasslands of the Falkland Islands. Not that I am a hermit – far from it. I enjoy people, but I also enjoy being alone – not just alone in a room or for a few hours on a beach, but truly alone, days and miles from the nearest human being. It is a heady experience that stretches senses and intensifies thoughts. It is only then that I can be wholly myself. 🍁

Bananas are much more versatile than you might imagine. Whether plain, baked, deep-fried or marinated, they taste just a little bit different every time. In this recipe, bananas are first marinated in rum and Canadian maple syrup and then fried.

Marinated bananas with hazelnuts and meringue

Halve the bananas lengthwise, leaving them in their skins. Transfer to an ovenproof dish, sprinkle with the salt and pour the rum and maple syrup over the top. Leave to marinate for 2 hours.

Coarsely chop the hazelnuts. Dry-roast the hazelnuts in a frying pan. Remove and set aside.

Place the marinated bananas in the frying pan, cut side down, and leave to caramelise over medium heat. Lightly crush the meringues. Serve 2 banana halves per person, sprinkled with toasted hazelnuts and the crushed meringues.

TIP This is delicious with vanilla ice cream.

Serves 4

4 bananas
1 pinch salt
100 ml (3½ fl oz) rum
4 tbsp maple syrup
4 tbsp hazelnuts
2–3 meringues

A North American classic with a Canadian twist, this cheese cake is made with maple syrup for a delectably distinctive flavour. If you prefer a milder maple flavour, use light-coloured syrup. Dark maple syrup has a much stronger taste, which gives the cake a slightly tart flavour that harmonises well with the sweet strawberries.

Maple cheesecake with strawberries

Makes one 26 cm (10½ inch) cheesecake

150 g (5½ oz) oatcakes
  (or use the crackers from
  p. 163)
⅔ cup (75 g) walnuts
90 g (3¼ oz) butter, softened,
  plus extra for greasing
1 pinch sea salt
750 g (1 lb 10 oz) cream
  cheese, softened
115 ml (3¾ fl oz) maple syrup,
  plus extra for serving
3 eggs

Also:
1⅔ cups (250 g) strawberries
2 tbsp lemon juice
1–2 tsp icing (confectioners)
  sugar

Preheat the oven to 180°C (350°F). Line the base of a 26 cm (10½ inch) springform tin with baking paper and lightly butter the side of the tin. Coarsely crush the biscuits. Transfer to a food processor with the walnuts and chop finely. Add the biscuits, nuts, butter and salt to a bowl and mix well. Press the mixture firmly into the tin.

Whisk the cream cheese. Stir in the maple syrup. Add the eggs, one at a time, and whisk to combine. Pour the mixture into the base and level the top.

Bake the cheesecake for 45–50 minutes. Remove from the oven, slide a knife around the side to loosen and leave to cool in the tin. Refrigerate the cooled cheesecake for 4 hours.

Wash, trim and quarter the strawberries. Gently toss with the lemon juice and icing sugar in a bowl and set aside to marinate briefly. Serve the cake with the strawberries and maple syrup.

Grilled lemonade

Wash and halve the lemons, place in a heated chargrill pan, cut side down, and grill briefly. Turn and allow the skins to take on colour as well. Remove from the pan and leave to cool briefly.

Add the sugar and 4 cups (1 litre) water to a large saucepan. Heat, stirring, until the sugar has dissolved. Juice the grilled lemons and add the juice to the pan. Remove from the heat and refrigerate.

Rinse the mint and shake off excess water. Add crushed ice to serving glasses, top up with the lemonade and serve garnished with mint leaves.

Makes about 4 cups (1 litre)

4 large lemons
200 g (7 oz) sugar
4 sprigs mint
Crushed ice

Caesar

Add the tomato juice, lime juice, vodka and Worcestershire sauce to a cocktail shaker and shake well.

Wash the lemon under hot water and slice into wedges. Moisten the rim of two tall glasses with a little water. Place the celery salt on a small plate and dip the rims of the glasses into the salt.

Add the lemon wedges and ice cubes to the glasses and fill up with the Caesar mixture. Serve garnished with the celery stalks.

Makes 2 glasses

400 ml (14 fl oz) tomato
  juice
Juice of 2 limes
100 ml (3½ fl oz) vodka
1 tsp Worcestershire sauce
1 lemon
Celery salt

Also:
Ice cubes
2 celery stalks

**Take
a walk
on the
wild side.**

Ingredients

A

Alfalfa sprouts 60, 138
Allspice 24
Almond butter 33
Almond milk 33, 52
Apple cider vinegar 27, 83, 114, 146
Apple juice 115, 119, 141, 152
Asparagus 60
Avocados 27

B

Bacon 42, 101, 123
Baguette 71, 127
Bananas 173
Basil 59, 149
Bay leaf 98, 141, 152, 158
Beans 149
Beef 75, 98, 134, 161
Beef bones 98
Berries 33, 38, 41, 52, 64, 124, 127, 174
Blackberries 33
Blackcurrant jam 115
Blueberries 33, 41, 52, 127
Bread 20, 64
Buttermilk 24, 141

C

Cabbage 141
Cajun spice mix 137, 161
Capers 101
Capsicum 134, 149
Caraway 75
Cardamom 45, 52, 123
Carrot 98, 134
Celeriac 98, 134
Celery 71, 177
Cheddar cheese 64, 72
Chicken 110, 155

Chicken stock 110
Chilli 115, 146
Chives 23, 60, 72, 138
Chocolate 30, 41, 45, 88, 120, 163
Chocolate hazelnut spread 80
Cinnamon 24, 33, 45, 52, 80, 123, 163
Cloves 24
Coconut milk 52
Coconut sugar 24
Cod 105
Coriander 158
Coriander seeds 141
Corn 102, 146
Cranberries 33, 52, 64, 124
Cranberry jam 64
Cranberry juice 124
Cream cheese 24, 138, 174
Curry powder 115, 141

D

Dark chocolate 30, 88, 120, 163
Desiccated coconut 88
Digestive biscuits 88

F

Fennel 105
Filo pastry 75
Fish 101, 105, 119, 138, 158
Fish stock 102, 105

G

Garlic 59, 71, 72, 98, 127, 134, 137, 141,
   146, 152, 161
Ghee 64
Ginger 24, 52
Goat's cheese 127
Gorgonzola 64

H

Halibut 101
Haloumi 98
Ham 23
Harissa 155
Hazelnuts 173
Honey 30, 71, 113, 115, 127, 146, 163

J

Jalapeños 64
Juniper berries 98, 134, 141, 152

L

Lamb's lettuce 113
Lard 123
Leek 75
Lemon 20, 71, 97, 101, 113, 119, 123,
   127, 138, 174, 177
Lemon thyme 113
Lettuce 101
Lime juice 146, 158, 177
Lobster 97

M

Macaroni 72
Mango 27
Maple syrup 33, 41, 52, 134, 152, 173, 174
Marshmallows 45, 163
Mayonnaise 60, 97, 101, 141, 146
Meringue 173
Milk chocolate 30, 88
Mint 177
Mushrooms 42, 110
Mussels/clams 102, 105
Mustard 110, 114, 115, 146

Ingredients

N

Nutmeg 24, 42, 45, 72

O

Oatcakes 174
Oats 30, 33
Onion 27, 42, 98, 134, 137, 149, 152, 155, 158

P

Pale ale 134
Parmesan 42, 72, 105, 165
Parsley 27, 42, 97, 98, 102, 138, 146
Peanut butter 30
Peanut oil 80
Pears 113
Pine needles 119
Pine nuts 113
Pork 75, 141
Potatoes 60, 97, 98, 102, 138, 161
Prawns 71, 105
Puff pastry 110
Pumpkin 24, 59

R

Radish 60
Raspberries 33, 38
Rice 42, 105
Ricotta 59
Risotto rice 105
Rosemary 42, 59, 119, 124, 127, 137, 149, 161
Rum 173

S

Salami 59
Salmon fillet 138, 158
Scallops 113
Smoking chips 119, 141
Sour cream 23, 138
Spare ribs 152
Spinach 59
Spring onions 110
Squid ink paste 101
Sriracha sauce 71
Strawberries 33, 174
Summer savoury 149

T

Thyme 59, 134, 137, 149
Tomatoes 23, 27, 59, 71, 98, 177
Tortillas 23
Trout 119

V

Vanilla 20, 24, 33, 38, 41, 52, 83, 88,
   123, 124, 163
Vodka 177

W

Walnuts 88, 174
Whisky 155
White chocolate 41, 45
Wild rice 42
Worcestershire sauce 71, 177

Y

Yeast 63, 80, 97, 123, 137
Yoghurt 60
Yufka pastry 75

Z

Zucchini 149

THERE IS A
WHOLE WORLD
OUT THERE

Recipes

A

Almond porridge with cranberry sauce 33

B

Baked potatoes with herbed sour cream
  and salmon 138
Barbecue sauce 115
Beaver bites 80
Berry latte 52
Blueberry pancakes with maple syrup 41
Breakfast wraps with scrambled eggs 23
Butter tarts 83

C

Caesar 177
Cauldron goulash with pale ale 134
Cedar plank salmon fillet 158
Chicken and mushroom pot pie 110
Chocolate pudding cake 120
Cinnamon scrolls with bacon 123
Clam chowder 102

F

French toast with lemon sugar 20

G

Grilled avocado with tomato chutney 27
Grilled cheese sandwich 64
Grilled corn with chipotle mayonnaise 146
Grilled lemonade 177

H

Home-made iced tea with cranberries 124

I

Ink-black halibut burgers 101

L

Lobster roll 97

M

Maple cheesecake with strawberries 174
Maple-glazed spare ribs 152
Marinated bananas with hazelnuts
  and meringue 173
Mayonnaise 114

N

Nanaimo bars 88
No-knead bread 63

O

One-pot mac & cheese 72
Onion campfire bread with Cajun spice
  butter 137

P

Pan-baked Bannock pizza 59
Peanut butter and chocolate granola 30
Pear salad with grilled scallops 113
Poutine 98
Prawn skewers with sriracha dip 71
Pulled pork burgers 141
Pumpkin spice muffins 24

R

Roast beef with smashed potatoes 161

S

Seafood risotto 105
Smoked trout 119
S'mores 163
Springtime potato salad 60

T

Toasted crostini with blueberries 127
Tourtière 75

W

Waffles with salted butterscotch sauce 38
Warm grilled vegetable salad 149
Whisky roast chicken 155
White hot chocolate 45
Wild rice frittata with mushrooms and bacon 42

The Team

Lisa Nieschlag

Lisa Nieschlag is a designer, cookbook author and food photographer.

Her beautifully produced photography has given many readers an appetite for more, especially when she also puts her immaculate styling credentials to effective use. The kitchen is the centre of Lisa's creative and culinary world.

Lisa writes the popular food blog "Liz & Jewels" together with Julia Cawley.

www.lizandjewels.com

Lars Wentrup

Lars Wentrup does it all: he's a designer, illustrator, gourmet and food taster. And he loves books.

Inspired by creative food styling and breathtaking photography, Lars creates a perfect platform that showcases good taste (both aesthetic and culinary) on paper.

Lars and Lisa have been running an agency for communication design in Munster since 2001.

www.nieschlag-und-wentrup.de

Sascha Talke

Sascha is not only a fitness guru and personal trainer, but also a passionate landscape and cityscape photographer. Whether at dawn or at midnight, he never shies away from any adventures to capture the perfect essence of the moment with his camera.

The results are rewarded with plenty of likes on Instagram.

Thanks

... to Sascha and Ninja, who spared no effort and went on many adventures to take the magnificent photos in Canada.

... to our set assistants, who supported us tirelessly in preparing and styling the many recipes:
Verena Poppen
Melissa and Sophie Lange
Nora Franzmeier

... to our cooperation partners for providing the beautiful decorations:
Geliebtes Zuhause
TineKHome
Taschenklub
Astrid Wallström Design PR
for Broste Copenhagen

Published in 2019 by Murdoch Books,
an imprint of Allen & Unwin
First published by Hölker Verlag in 2019

Murdoch Books Australia
83 Alexander Street Crows Nest NSW 2065
Phone: +61 (0)2 8425 0100
murdochbooks.com.au
info@murdochbooks.com.au

Murdoch Books UK
Ormond House, 26–27 Boswell Street, London WC1N 3JZ
Phone: +44 (0) 20 8785 5995
murdochbooks.co.uk
info@murdochbooks.co.uk

For corporate orders & custom publishing,
contact our business development team at
salesenquiries@murdochbooks.com.au.

Recipe development: Verena Poppen
Design and typesetting: Nieschlag + Wentrup, Büro für
Gestaltung | www.nieschlag-und-wentrup.de
Photos: Lisa Nieschlag: Pages 8, 10, 21, 22, 23, 25, 26, 27,
30, 31, 32, 33, 38, 39, 40, 42, 43, 44, 45, 47, 48, 52, 53, 58,
59, 60, 61, 62, 63, 65, 70, 73, 74, 75, 79, 81, 82, 83, 88, 89, 96,
97, 98, 99, 100, 102, 103, 104, 111, 112, 113, 114, 118, 120, 121,
122, 123, 124, 125, 126, 127, 134, 135, 136, 137, 139, 140, 141,
146, 147, 148, 152, 153, 154, 155, 159, 160, 161, 162, 163, 172,
173, 174, 175, 176, 177, 190
Sascha Talke: Pages 1, 4, 8, 11, 12, 13, 14, 15, 16, 18, 19, 28, 29,
34, 35, 36, 46, 50, 54, 56, 57, 66, 68, 69, 76, 78, 85, 86, 87,
90, 92, 94, 95, 106, 107, 108, 116, 117, 128, 129, 130, 132, 142,
143, 145, 150, 151, 156, 157, 164, 166, 168, 169, 170, 178, 179,
180, 186, 187, 191
Niklas Birkemeyer: Portrait p. 190, bottom left
Anna Haas: Portrait p. 190, top right
Ninja Talke: Portrait p. 8, top right
Friederike Wentrup: Portrait p. 8, bottom right
Shutterstock, PlusONE / Calin Tatu: Forest cover photo
Shutterstock, PlusONE: Pages 6, 7
Illustrations: Lars Wentrup
Editor: Franziska Grünewald
Prepress: FSM Premedia, Munster

Publisher: Corinne Roberts
Translator: Claudia McQuillan-Koch
English-language editor: Justine Harding
Production director: Lou Playfair

© 2019 Hölker Verlag, in Coppenrath Verlag GmbH & Co.
KG Hafenweg 30, 48155 Munster, Germany
All rights reserved, excepting text extracts.
www.hoelker-verlag.de

ISBN 978 1 76052 476 0 Australia
ISBN 978 1 91163 232 0 UK

A cataloguing-in-publication entry is available
from the catalogue of the National Library of
Australia at nla.gov.au.

A catalogue record for this book is available from the
British Library.
Printed in China by C&C Offset Printing Co. Ltd.

Text extracts:
Excerpt from CABIN AT SINGING RIVER by Chris
Czajkowski © Raincoast Books, 1991, Vancouver.
Reproduced with permission.

Excerpt from FUGITIVE PIECES by Anne Michaels © 1996
by Anne Michaels. Used in the US by permission of Alfred
A. Knopf, an imprint of the Knopf Doubleday Publishing
Group, a division of Penguin Random House LLC. Used in
Canada by permission of Emblem/McClelland & Stewart, a
division of Penguin Random House LLC. All rights reserved.
Used in the UK by permission of Bloomsbury Publishing plc.
All rights reserved.

Excerpt from "Uncles" from WILDERNESS TIPS by
Margaret Atwood © 1991 by O.W. Toad Limited. Used in the
US by permission of Doubleday, an imprint of the Knopf
Doubleday Publishing Group, a division of Penguin Random
House LLC. Used in Canada by permission of Emblem/
McClelland & Stewart, a division of Penguin Random
House LLC. Used in the UK by permission of Bloomsbury
Publishing plc. All rights reserved.

Locations
Pyramid Lake, Jasper National Park: Pages 1, 12, 92
Maligne Lake, Jasper National Park: Pages 4, 56, 130, 168
Lynn Canyon Park, Vancouver: Page 11
Moraine Lake, Banff National Park: Pages 13, 50, 90, 187
Sunwapta Falls, Jasper National Park: Page 14
Athabasca Falls, Jasper National Park: Pages 15, 28
Two Jack Lake, Banff National Park: Pages 16, 191
Stanley Park, Vancouver: Page 18
Cascade Mountain, Banff National Park: Page 19
Capilano Suspension Bridge Park, Vancouver: Pages 29 (top),
87, 156, 157
Howe Sound, Vancouver: Page 29 (bottom)
Natural Bridge, Yoho National Park: Pages 34, 94
Tunnel Mountain Road, Banff National Park: Page 36
Myra Canyon, Kelowna: Page 46
Icefields Parkway, Jasper National Park: Page 54
Mount Bundle, Banff National Park: Pages 66, 116, 169
Lake Louise, Banff National Park: Pages 57 (top), 85
Lake Minnewanka, Banff National Park: Pages 57 (bottom), 117, 129
(bottom), 186
Emerald Lake, Yoho National Park: Pages 76, 144 (Lodge)
Mount Edith Cavell, Jasper National Park: Page 78
Bow River, Banff National Park: Page 86
Johnston Canyon, Banff National Park: Pages 106, 107
Peyton Lake, Banff National Park: Page 108
Shannon Falls, Provincial Park, Vancouver: Pages 128, 178, 179, 180
Jasper National Park: Pages 132, 166
Vermilion Lakes, Banff National Park: Page 142
Lynn Canyon, Vancouver: Pages 150, 151
Fairmont Hotel, Banff National Park: Page 164
Columbia River, Revelstoke National Park: Page 170